中国人的生活故事

（第二辑）三十而立

Stories of Chinese People's Lives Ⅱ

People in Their 30s

孔子学院总部/国家汉办 编

外语教学与研究出版社
FOREIGN LANGUAGE TEACHING AND RESEARCH PRESS
北京 BEIJING

图书在版编目（CIP）数据

中国人的生活故事. 第二辑. 三十而立 / 孔子学院总部 / 国家汉办编. —— 北京：外语教学
与研究出版社，2016.9（2023.7 重印）
ISBN 978-7-5135-8139-4

I. ①中… II. ①孔… III. ①汉语－阅读教学－对外汉语教学－自学参考资料 IV. ①H195.4

中国版本图书馆 CIP 数据核字（2016）第 235027 号

出 版 人　王　芳
项目策划　郑丽慧　李　丹
责任编辑　向凤菲
英文编辑　张立萍
装帧设计　姚　军
出版发行　外语教学与研究出版社
社　　址　北京市西三环北路 19 号（100089）
网　　址　https://www.fltrp.com
印　　刷　北京盛通印刷股份有限公司
开　　本　787×1092　1/24
印　　张　7
版　　次　2016 年 10 月第 1 版　2023 年 7 月第 2 次印刷
书　　号　ISBN 978-7-5135-8139-4
定　　价　49.00 元

如有图书采购需求，图书内容或印刷装订等问题，侵权、盗版书籍等线索，请拨打以下电话或关注官方服务号：
客服电话：400 898 7008
官方服务号：微信搜索并关注公众号"外研社官方服务号"
外研社购书网址：https://fltrp.tmall.com

物料号：281390001

记载人类文明
沟通世界文化
www.fltrp.com

出版说明

　　为满足海内外汉语学习者对汉语读物的需求，促进中外文化交流与了解，孔子学院总部/国家汉办继2015年策划、出版了《中国人的生活故事》（第一辑）之后，又启动了《中国人的生活故事》（第二辑）的编写、出版项目。

　　《中国人的生活故事》（第二辑）旨在通过讲述各行各业的普通中国人的一天，向各国汉语学习者展现平凡、真实又温暖人心的当代中国人的生活，介绍历史悠久又与时俱进的中国传统文化。

　　本系列读物共有7个分册，分别为：《弱冠桃李》《三十而立》《四十不惑》《五十知命》《六十花甲》《七十古稀》《耄耋之年》，呈现了从二十岁左右的年轻人到八九十岁的耄耋老人的生活状态和精神风貌。

　　本系列读物主要具有以下特色：

　　1.选文内容真实、语言地道。每个分册收录6篇选文，均取材于腾讯网《中国人的一天》栏目，讲述6个民族、地区、职业等各不相同的人物的故事，以满足不同读者群体的阅读需求。

　　2.每篇选文标注对应的HSK等级。根据生词、句长、文化点等的不同，将选文难度标为HSK4级到HSK6级不等，为不同汉语水平的读者提供参考。

　　3.生词选择以《HSK考试大纲》中的"词汇大纲"为依据。选文生词以超纲词、HSK6级词、HSK5级词为主，重点难点词筛选后随文附注，提供相应的词性与英文释义。书后附有全书生词索引，方便读者查阅。

4.注重中国传统文化与当代中国风貌的呈现。文中具有文化特色的词语和网络流行用语随文单独列出，提供详细的中英文解释说明；每篇选文后设置"延伸阅读"板块，以中英文对照阅读的形式向读者进一步介绍与主题相关的文化事物和现象。

5.全书图文并茂，可读性强。选文正文配有相应的真实摄影照片，文化词汇的解释以及"延伸阅读"等板块也视需要提供配图，帮助读者更直观、形象地理解相应的文字说明。

6.注重阅读的趣味性和互动性。每篇选文后设置"文化链接"板块，提供和选文主题相关的文化练习或趣味活动。

《中国人的生活故事》（第二辑）系列读物精读、泛读皆宜，既可用于辅助教师课堂教学，也适合学习者课外阅读学习。希望本系列读物可以为海内外的汉语学习者打开一扇了解当代中国之窗，也希望读者通过阅读本系列图书加深对中国经济、社会、民俗、地理的了解，学习到全新、鲜活、实用的汉语。

外语教学与研究出版社
2016年9月

Publisher's Note

To satisfy the demand for reading materials for Chinese learners at home and abroad and to promote intercultural communication and understanding, the Confucius Institute Headquarters (Hanban) has commissioned the compilation and publication of the second series of *Stories of Chinese People's Lives*, after the publication of its first series in 2015.

Through descriptions of an ordinary day for Chinese people from all walks of life, the second series of *Stories of Chinese People's Lives* aims to share real and heartwarming life stories from contemporary Chinese people and to introduce the ancient and yet constantly evolving Chinese culture to Chinese learners worldwide.

This series contains seven books: *People in Their 20s*, *People in Their 30s*, *People in Their 40s*, *People in Their 50s*, *People in Their 60s*, *People in Their 70s*, and *People in Their 80s and 90s*. These books serve to illustrate the daily lives and outlooks of people of all ages.

The second series of *Stories of Chinese People's Lives* has the following features:

1. Texts in each book are true stories written in authentic Chinese. Each book includes six texts, all of which are drawn from the *One Day, One Life* column on QQ.com. To satisfy the interests of different and diverse groups of readers, each book tells the stories of six people from various ethnic groups, regions and professions.

2. Each text corresponds to a specific HSK level. Based on its vocabulary, sentence length and cultural elements, each text is marked between HSK 4 and HSK 6 as a reference for learners at different levels.

3. The key words in each text are selected based on the vocabulary syllabus in the *HSK Test Syllabus*, and are mainly composed of words at or above HSK 5 and HSK 6. These key words are listed alongside the text and parts of speech and

definitions are explained in English. A glossary is attached at the end of each book for the readers' reference.

4. The presentation of both traditional and contemporary Chinese culture is equally stressed. Words containing cultural elements and Internet buzzwords are highlighted and illustrated alongside the text with detailed annotations in both Chinese and English. Each text is followed by a reading section called Extensive Reading, which contains a further bilingual introduction of related cultural events or phenomena.

5. Each book is made very readable with attractive pictures and well-written texts. Real life photos are correspondingly arranged on every page of the texts. The words containing cultural elements and the Extended Reading passages are also complimented with pictures to make them more visually engaging.

6. The books stress an amusing and interactive reading experience. A Cultural Links section is set in each text, providing cultural exercises or interesting activities related to the themes of the texts.

The second series of *Stories of Chinese People's Lives* is applicable to both intensive and extensive reading. The books can be used as classroom materials for teachers and also as extra-curricular reading materials for Chinese learners. We hope that this series of books will open a window for Chinese learners, both at home and abroad, to learn more about contemporary China. We also hope that reading these books will help learners to deepen their understanding of China's economy, society, traditional customs, and geography; as well gain a modern, fresh and useful Chinese vocabulary.

Foreign Language Teaching and Research Press
September, 2016

生词词性缩略形式表

英文缩写	英文全称	中文名称
n.	noun	名词
p.n.	proper noun	专有名词
v.	verb	动词
adj.	adjective	形容词
num.	numeral	数词
m.	measure word	量词
pron.	pronoun	代词
adv.	adverb	副词
prep.	preposition	介词
conj.	conjunction	连词
part.	particle	助词
int.	interjection	叹词
ono.	onomatopoeic word	拟声词

目录 CONTENTS

记忆中的年
Spring Festival from Memory

每一个中国人都拥有一份独特的关于过年的记忆。

Every Chinese has his or her unique memory of celebrating the Spring Festival.

"影痴"刘老师
Mr Liu: A Teacher and Devoted Cineaste

一位 80 后资深电影爱好者坚定地追寻着他的电影梦。

A post-1980s devoted cineaste is firmly pursuing his film dream.

"红绣轩主"
"Master of the Red Embroidery Chamber"

35 岁的杨小婷是中国非物质文化遗产汉绣的带头人。

35-year-old Yang Xiaoting is a leading expert of China's intangible cultural heritage Han embroidery.

Jiā lǐ duō le gè mèimei

家里多了个妹妹

A Younger Sister Came to the Family

2008年，袁野和毕野的第一个孩子米多出生；2014年，34岁的袁野和妻子迎来了他们的第二个女儿。

In 2008, Miduo, the first child of Yuan Ye and Bi Ye was born; and in 2014, 34-year-old Yuan Ye and his wife welcomed their second daughter.

2014年10月16日，在外地出差的袁野起早赶回沈阳，到医院陪护临产的妻子。34岁的袁野和妻子毕野，名字相近而且同龄。袁野有一个同胞哥哥，妻子毕野是独生子女。2008年，夫妻俩第一个孩子袁梓馨（乳名"米多"）出生。2014年，二女儿米乐的到来改变了原来一家三口的家庭模式。

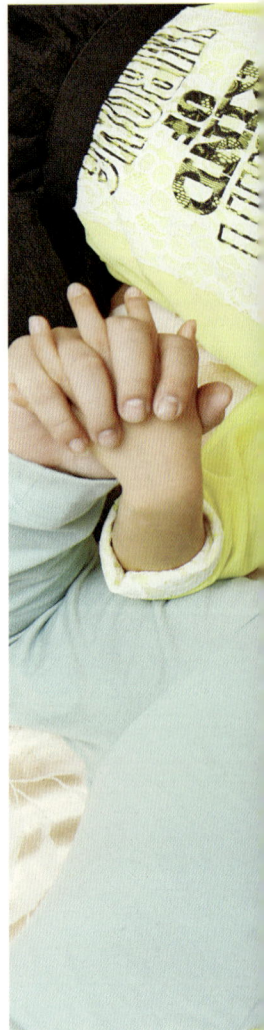

陪护	péihù	v.	accompany and look after
临产	línchǎn	v.	be about to give birth
同胞	tóngbāo	n.	sibling
独生子女	dúshēng zǐnǚ		only child
夫妻	fūqī	n.	husband and wife
袁梓馨	Yuán Zǐxīn	p.n.	name of a person
乳名	rǔmíng	n.	infant name
满月	mǎnyuè	v.	(of a baby) be one month old

2014年11月16日，刚刚满月的二女儿米乐和家人合影。

作为独生子女，毕野想要给孩子提供一个有兄弟姐妹陪伴的成长环境。

2013年，国家出台了新政策，提出坚持计划生育的基本国策，实施一方是独生子女的夫妇可以生育两个孩子的政策，逐步调整和完善生育政策，促进人口长期均衡发展。

兄弟姐妹	xiōngdì jiěmèi		brothers and sisters; siblings
陪伴	péibàn	v.	keep sb company
出台	chūtái	v.	(of a policy, measure, etc) come out; unveil
计划生育	jìhuà shēngyù		family planning
国策	guócè	n.	state/national policy
方	fāng	n.	side; party
均衡	jūnhéng	adj.	balanced; proportionate

2014年4月10日，袁野夫妇在人口和计划生育部门办理了生育二胎的手续。

　　中国自20世纪80年代实施提倡一对夫妻生育一个孩子的计划生育政策以来，两个大人一个小孩逐渐成为了最常见的家庭组合。而近年来，随着生育政策的放开，这样的小家庭模式正在慢慢改变。

二胎	èrtāi	n.	second child
大人	dàren	n.	adult; grown-up
组合	zǔhé	n.	combination
放开	fàngkāi	v.	loosen
产前	chǎnqián	n.	prenatal period

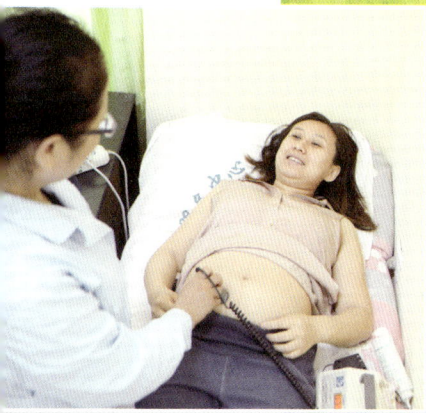

毕野在医院里做产前检查。

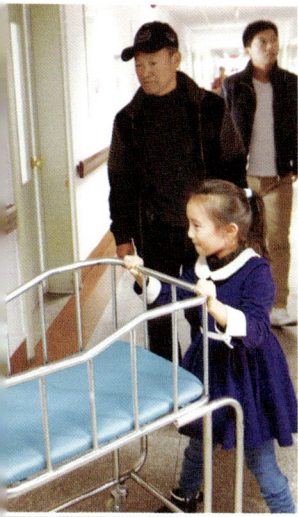

　　妹妹出生时，小米多像是个小大人儿似的，跟在爸爸身后，帮着推婴儿车。

　　"小妹妹肉乎乎的，挺沉的。"姐姐说。

　　"希望孩子健康成长，虽然辛苦一些，但很值得。"妈妈说。

　　"多一个伴儿，孩子长大以后不孤单。"爸爸说。

　　"赶上国家新政策了，我又多了一个外孙女。"姥姥说。

小大人儿	xiǎodàrénr	n.	child talking or behaving like an adult
肉乎乎	ròuhūhū	adj.	chubby
沉	chén	adj.	heavy (in weight)
伴儿	bànr	n.	companion
孤单	gūdān	adj.	alone; lonely
赶上	gǎnshàng	v.	be in time for
外孙女	wàisūnnǚ	n.	daughter's daughter; granddaughter

米多有时也想抱抱小妹妹。

妹妹米乐睡着了，米多还想再逗她玩一会儿。

逗　　**dòu**　　*v.*　　tease; kid

米乐在妈妈的怀里睡得很香甜。妈妈爱抚着她的小脚丫。

香甜	xiāngtián	*adj.*	sound (sleep)
爱抚	àifǔ	*v.*	show tender care of
脚丫	jiǎoyā	*n.*	foot

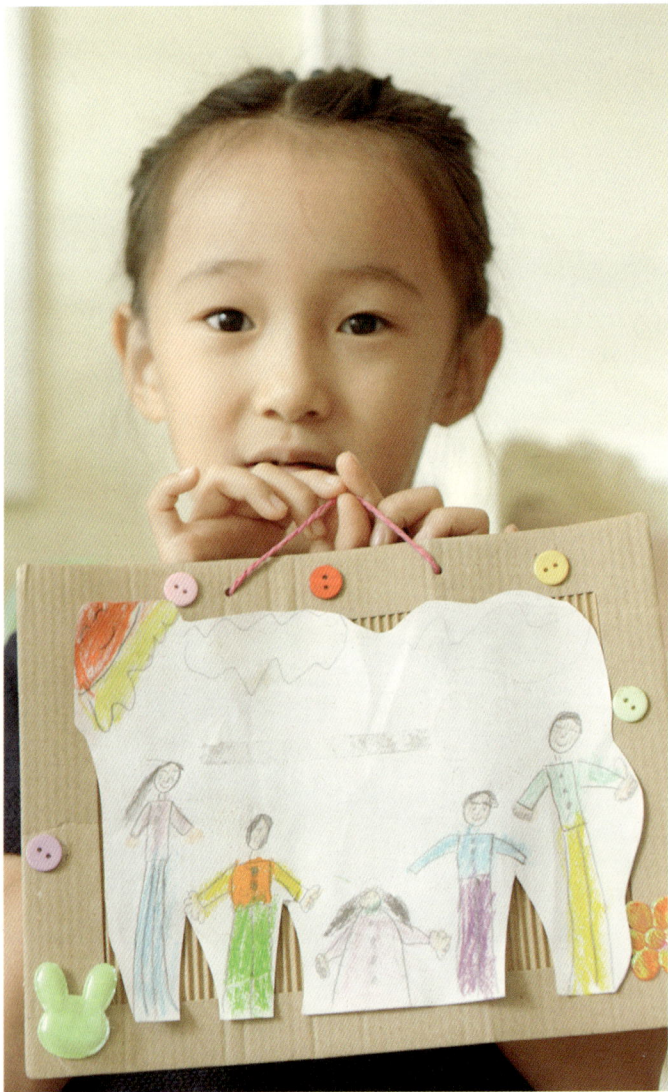

袁梓馨画的图画里，有姥姥、姥爷、妈妈、爸爸和自己，这种家庭组合正在发生改变。

| 姥爷 | **lǎoye** | *n.* | (maternal) grandfather |
| 舞台 | **wǔtái** | *n.* | stage; arena |

生育政策放开以后，一对夫妻一个孩子的独生子女时代将成为历史，**独生子女父母光荣证**也将退出历史舞台。

（本文选编自腾讯网《中国人的一天》栏目，

作者：蔡敏强。）

● 独生子女父母光荣证

dúshēng zǐnǚ fùmǔ guāngróngzhèng

国家发给自愿终身只生育一个子女的夫妻的荣誉证书。获得此证书的夫妻，按照有关规定，可享受独生子女父母奖励。

The state issues a "Certificate of Honour for Single-child Parents" to couples who are willing to have only one child in their lifetime. According to related regulations, couples with such certificate are entitled to corresponding rewards.

中国的计划生育政策

China's Family Planning Policy

　　20 世纪五六十年代，中国政府主张"人多力量大"，民众也认为多子多福，因此人口快速增长。之后，国家逐步把计划生育定为基本国策，开始控制人口增长。

　　从 20 世纪 70 年代提倡"一个不少，两个正好，三个多了"，到 80 年代施行提倡一对夫妇只生育一个孩子的独生子女政策，从 2013 年实施一方是独生子女的夫妇可生育两个孩子的单独两孩政策，到 2015 年提出全面实施一对夫妇可生育两个孩子的全面两孩政策，再到 2021 年实施一对夫妇可以生育三个孩子的政策，中国的生育政策始终在不断调整和完善。

　　当前，中国 15～30 岁的独生子女人数众多。全面两孩政策的推行意味着中国实施了 30 多年的独生子女政策正式宣告终结。在这几十年中，中国的家庭结构逐渐从传统的大家庭变为"421 家庭"（四名祖父母和外祖父母、两名父母、一名独生子女）。中国的独生子女一代，曾被指责为娇气任性、以自我为中心。如今，走入而立之年的他们，都承担起了结婚生子、赡养父母的责任。由于工作忙、压力大等原因，许多独生子

女夫妻将孩子交给父母照顾，"隔代抚养"非常普遍。而面对父母的衰老，很多独生子女都感叹，父母养老问题负担不轻！

近年来，中国人口生育率下降也带来了一些令人始料未及的问题，如老年人口数量不断上升，男女比例失衡等。为应对这些问题，计划生育政策逐渐放开，新政策相继出台，配套支持措施也日趋完善。

In the 1950s and 1960s, the Chinese government asserted that "many hands make light work", and Chinese people believed that more blessings came with more offspring, which led to a surge in China's population. Thereafter, China made family planning a basic state policy step by step to rein in the population growth.

In the 1970s, "one child, good; two children, sufficient; and three children, too many" was advocated, and in the 1980s, the one-child policy which advocated one child for one couple was adopted. In 2013, the policy relaxed to allow couples with any side being an only child to have two children. In 2015, the universal two-child policy which allowed all couples nation-wide to have two children was formulated. Then in 2021, the policy which allowed couples to have three children was implemented. This evolution demonstrates that China's family planning policies are being adjusted and improved constantly.

Presently, China has a large number of only children between 15 to 30 years old. The implementation of the universal two-child policy declared a formal end to the one-child policy which had been carried out for over three decades. During the past decades, Chinese family structure has gradually changed from the traditional big family into the "four-two-one family" (four grandparents, two parents and one only child). The Chinese one-child generation was once criticised as capricious and self-centred. Now, in their 30s, they have shouldered the obligations to get married, give birth, and take care of their parents. Many of them ask their parents to care for their children due to busy work and high pressure. So skip-generation raising is widely seen. Facing the aging of their parents, many of the one-child generation think that the burden to provide for their parents is not light.

In recent years, China's declining fertility rate has led to some unexpected issues, such as ever-growing aging population and imbalanced sex ratio. To address these issues, family planning policy has been gradually loosened up, new policies have been introduced, and supporting measures are also becoming increasingly perfect.

根据"延伸阅读"的文章，回答以下问题。

Answer the following questions according to the text in the "Extensive Reading".

1. 中国的计划生育政策经历了哪些变化？

What changes has China's family planning policy undergone?

2. 近年来，中国为什么逐渐放开了计划生育政策？

Why has China gradually relaxed its family planning policy in recent years?

3. 你们国家的生育政策是什么？请介绍一下。

What is your country's fertility policy? Please introduce it.

4. 你认为独生子女好还是有兄弟姐妹好？请在下表中列举二者的优缺点。

Do you think it is better to have an only child or to have siblings? Please list the advantages and disadvantages of both in the form below.

	优点 advantages	缺点 disadvantages
独生子女 have an only child		
有兄弟姐妹 have siblings		

Kuàidì   xiǎogēr   de   "Gòuwùjié"

快递小哥儿的"购物节"

"Shopping Festival" for the Courier

近年来，中国的网购势头发展迅猛，物流业也随之兴盛。张锐做快递员已经五六年了，每年的网络"购物节"是他最忙碌的时候。

Recent years have seen a rapid increase in China's online shopping, which contributed considerably to the boom of the logistics industry. Zhang Rui has been working as a courier for five or six years. The annual online "Shopping Festival" is his busiest time of the year.

近年来，随着各互联网电商"购物节"的到来，网络购物蓬勃兴起，这也影响着物流业的发展。张锐是扬州市一家快递公司的快递员，从事快递行业已有五六年。11月的"双十一购物节"期间，他每天都会打出近百个重复的电话："您好，您的快递到了，我在您楼下……"

● 双十一购物节
Shuāngshíyī Gòuwùjié
"双十一购物节"始于2009年，是以阿里巴巴为代表的电商平台于每年的11月11日推出的大型购物促销活动。
Started in 2009, the "Double 11 Shopping Festival" is a large-scale sales promotion launched by e-commerce platforms represented by Alibaba in China on 11th November each year.

电商	diànshāng	n.	e-business; e-commerce
蓬勃	péngbó	adj.	flourishing; thriving
兴起	xīngqǐ	v.	rise; spring up
物流业	wùliúyè	n.	logistics industry
扬州	Yángzhōu	p.n.	a city in Jiangsu Province
快递	kuàidì	n.	special/express delivery

初冬的扬州，室外天气很冷，快递员张锐正在抹护肤霜。他在为即将开始的一天做准备。

创可贴、护肤霜和感冒药是张锐冬天的随身"三件宝"。

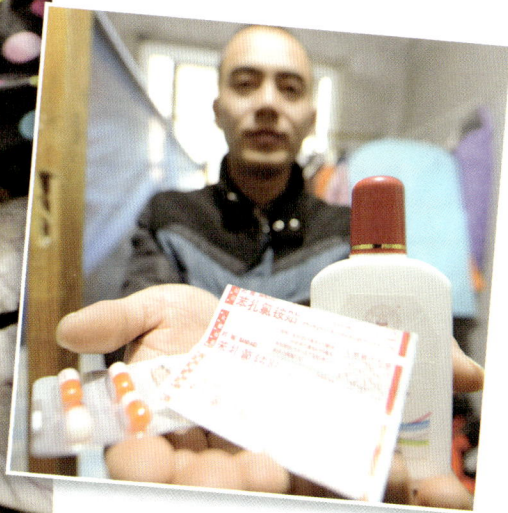

室外	shìwài	n.	outside of a building
抹	mǒ	v.	apply; put on
护肤霜	hùfūshuāng	n.	face cream; body lotion
创可贴	chuāngkětiē	n.	Band-Aid

因为赶时间，上班途中，张锐在路边买了点儿早餐，边走边吃。"购物节"期间，他每天要跑近50公里路程，送150件快件，从早上七点一直忙到晚上十点多。

近期，"购物节"一个接着一个，各大快递公司才刚刚经历完"双十一"，又要为即将到来的"双十二购物节"做准备了。

路程	lùchéng	n.	distance travelled; journey
快件	kuàijiàn	n.	express mail/delivery
近期	jìnqī	n.	near future; recent days

张锐在上交当天的快件回单。

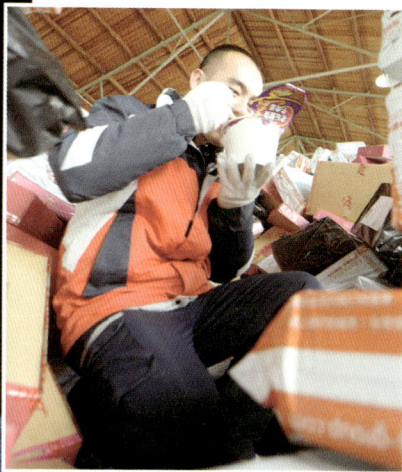

张锐利用派件间隙吃了一碗泡面。他的早饭和午饭几乎都在电动车上解决，晚上十点多回家后才吃"正餐"。他笑着说："送完一天的快件后，脸都冻麻木了。"

派件	pàijiàn	v.	ship; deliver
间隙	jiànxì	n.	interval; gap
泡面	pàomiàn	n.	instant noodles
电动车	diàndòngchē	n.	electric vehicle
正餐	zhèngcān	n.	regular meal
上交	shàngjiāo	v.	hand in; submit
回单	huídān	n.	receipt

发工资后，张锐会习惯性地去银行查看自己的账户。据了解，在"购物节"期间，快递员的月收入基本都会成倍增长。张锐说："这样的网上'购物节'，对于我们这些快递员来说，真是个甜蜜的'负担'。"

习惯性	xíguànxìng	n.	habituation
查看	chákàn	v.	check; see about
据	jù	prep.	according to
甜蜜	tiánmì	adj.	sweet; happy

完成一天的工作时已经是凌晨，张锐在寒风中骑着车回出租屋。由于老家不在扬州，张锐不能经常回去。特别是到每年"购物节"时，他就不得不延迟回家的时间。

张锐有一个5岁的可爱儿子，每当他因工作没有时间回家时，儿子就会要求妈妈带自己坐城际公交到扬州找爸爸。

寒风	hánfēng	n.	cold/bleak wind
延迟	yánchí	v.	delay; postpone
每当	měidāng	prep.	whenever; every time
城际	chéngjì	adj.	intercity
公交	gōngjiāo	n.	public transport

凌晨，张锐回到家后下了一碗鸡蛋面，开始吃他一天当中的"正餐"。

吃完以后，张锐用热水泡脚解乏。只有在这个时候，他才能坐下来享受一下生活。

下	xià	v.	put into; cook
当中	dāngzhōng	n.	centre; middle
泡脚	pàojiǎo	v.	soak feet in warm water
解乏	jiěfá	v.	recover from fatigue
享受	xiǎngshòu	v.	enjoy

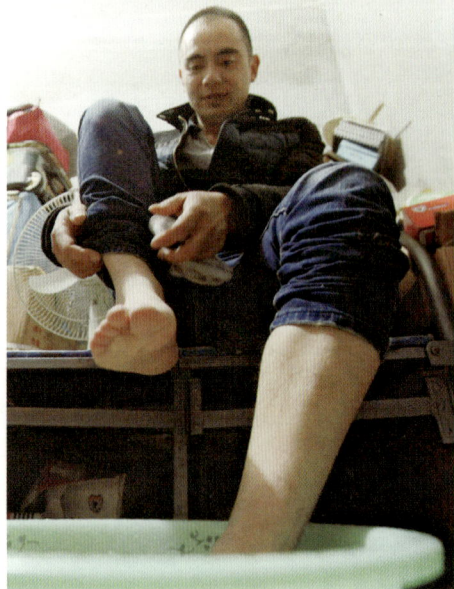

睡觉前，张锐给自己简单地做了一下头部按摩，缓解疲劳。他还会打开手机查看第二天的天气。

头部	tóubù	n.	head
按摩	ànmó	v.	massage
缓解	huǎnjiě	v.	alleviate; ease up
疲劳	píláo	adj.	tired; fatigued

张锐和他的同事们都是一群有梦想的年轻人。当谈到自己的梦想时，张锐笑着说："希望将来可以有自己的生意，当一个老板。"

（本文选编自腾讯网《中国人的一天》栏目，作者：孟德龙。）

| 梦想 | mèngxiǎng | n. | dream |
| 老板 | lǎobǎn | n. | boss |

"双十一":人造血拼狂欢节

"Double 11": The Man-made Shopping Festival

2009 年 11 月 11 日,"天猫"(当时称"淘宝商城")开始在"光棍节"举办促销活动,希望可以通过促销推广品牌。而这个人造的网络购物节自诞生之日起,就火得一发不可收拾。

目前,"双十一"已经被消费者当作一年中最好的囤货时机。这一天,电商平台上平时不打折的商品也会打 4 ~ 5 折,甚至是 2 ~ 3 折。充满诱惑力的优惠使得"剁手党"们目不转睛地盯着自己的电脑或手机屏幕,生怕晚了一步,就错过这难得的大好机会。

2022 年是第 14 届"双十一"。根据公布的数据,这一年"双十一"期间全网交易额突破 5571 亿元。天猫"双十一"活动开始仅一个小时,102 个品牌成交额便已过亿。11 月 12 日,国家邮政局发布的数据显示,"双十一"当天全国快递处理量达 5.52 亿件,是日常业务量水平的 1.8 倍。

如今，"双十一"已经成为购物节的代名词。它不仅是网购族们的狂欢，对非网购人群、线下商城也产生了很大的影响。现在，"双十一"已经从天猫扩展到几乎所有电商平台，从中国扩展到全球。11月11日正逐渐从单一的电商营销日，变为大部分消费者的购物狂欢节。

On 11 November, 2009, Tmall (then known as the "Taobao Mall") started promotional campaigns on the Singles' Day, hoping to promote their brands through sales promotion. Since then, this man-made online shopping festival has been gaining momentum.

"Double 11" now is regarded as the best hoarding time by consumers. On this day, e-commerce platforms offer discounts of up to 50% to 60% off, or even 70% to 80% off for goods with no discounts on regular days. The attractive discounts keep online shoppers or "shopaholics" fixing their eyes on the computer or smartphone's screen, just in case they would miss this rare opportunity.

2022 marks the 14th "Double 11" shopping festival. According to the official data, the total transaction volume during this year's "Double 11" period exceeded 557.1 billion *yuan*. Within just one hour after the start of Tmall's "Double 11" event, the sales volume of 102 brands had already surpassed 100 million *yuan*. On November 12th, data released by the State Post Bureau showed that the total volume of express deliveries nationwide on the "Double 11" day reached 552 million parcels, which is 1.8 times the normal daily volume. "Parcels are up to my ears", a courier posted on his Weibo account.

Today, "Double 11" has become a synonym for shopping festivals. It is not only a holiday for online shoppers, but also has an impact on people who do not shop online and brick and mortar

shopping malls. Nowadays, "Double 11" has spread from Tmall to almost all e-commerce platforms, and from China to the whole world. It is gradually growing from an online retailers' marketing day to a shopping carnival for most consumers.

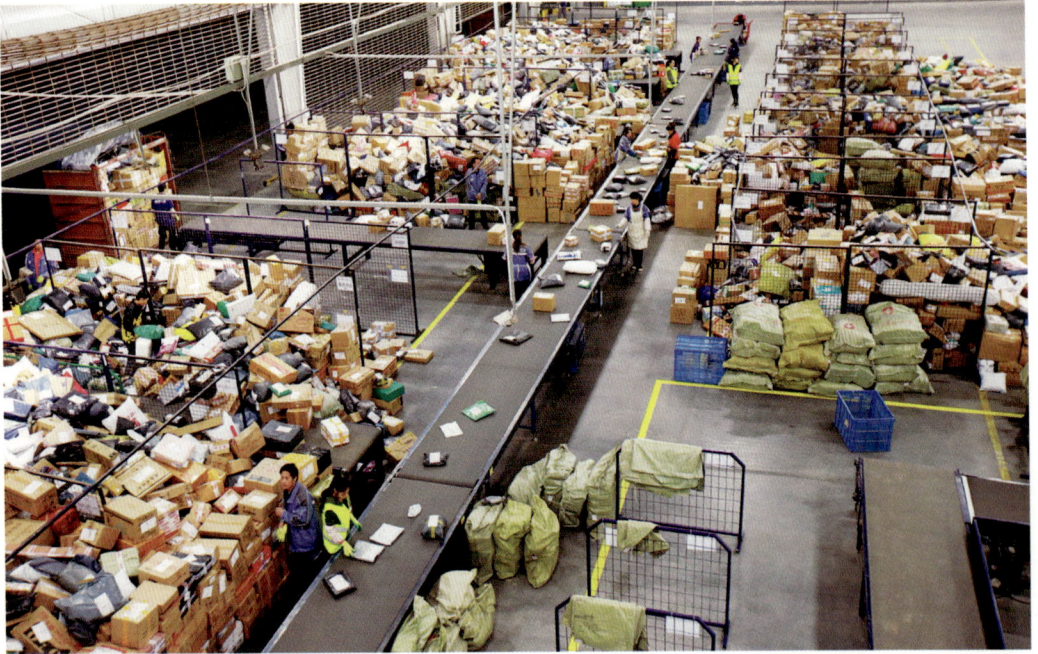

文化链接 Cultural Links

一、猜一猜下面这些与"购物和消费"相关的流行语是什么意思，并写出一个目前在中国正在流行的网络词语。

Guess the meaning of the following popular phrases related to shopping and consumption, and provide an example of an Internet slang currently trending in China.

光棍节：_____

（提示：这个节日在每年11月11日。）

(Hint: This festival is celebrated on November 11th each year.)

月光族：_____

（提示："月光"的意思是"每个月都花光"。）

(Hint: The phrase "月光" means "spending all of one's monthly income".)

剁手党：_____

（提示："剁手"的意思是"砍掉自己的手"。）

(Hint: The phrase "剁手" literally means "chopping off one's own hand".)

再写一个网络流行语：_____

Please write down another Internet slang.

二、在你们国家，有和"双十一"类似的购物节吗？如果有，它和中国的"双十一"有什么异同？

Do you have a similar shopping festival like "Double 11" in your country? If so, what are the similarities and differences between it and China's "Double 11"?

Àibǐbān   de shuāngmiàn shēnghuó

艾 比 班 的 双 面 生 活

The Double Life of Habibe

艾比班·热合木是新疆维吾尔自治区的一名教师，同时她还是多家馕店的创始者。她希望传播新疆馕的传统文化，让更多人了解馕的医疗价值。

Habibe Rahim is a teacher in Xinjiang Uygur Autonomous Region, and she is also a founder of several naan stores. She wants to spread the traditional culture of Xinjiang naan so that more people can be familiar with its medical values.

1996年，艾比班·热合木从新疆师范大学毕业，成了伊宁市第十五小学的一名教师。

2015年7月，记者在新疆伊宁见到了艾比班。她身穿一袭粉衣，干练大方，散发着知性又亲切的气息。

袭	xí	m.	a suit or set of clothes
干练	gànliàn	adj.	capable and experienced
知性	zhīxìng	n.	intellectuality
气息	qìxī	n.	smell; flavour; scent

艾比班在看学生的画儿。

艾比班虽然没有上过汉语学校，却说着一口流利的汉语。因为父亲曾在伊犁州教育局工作，艾比班从小就在第十五小学后面的教育局**家属院**长大，有很多汉族发小。她最好的朋友是汉族邻居欧洋。她回忆说，欧洋的数学很好，小时候遇到不会解的数学题，都是欧洋帮忙。

现在欧洋是一名幼儿园教师，三十年来，两人的联系从未间断，现在还经常在一起探讨教学问题。

● 家属院 *jiāshǔyuàn*

在城镇中，一些单位给职工安排居住的住宅区，在这个区域里居住的基本都是该单位的员工及其家属。

In urban areas, some work units provide accommodation for their employees, so such residential communities are home to staff members and their family mostly.

发小	fàxiǎo	*n.*	childhood buddy
解题	jiětí	*v.*	solve a (mathematical, etc) problem
间断	jiànduàn	*v.*	be disconnected
教学	jiàoxué	*n.*	teaching; education

艾比班还有另一个身份——伊宁市西帕伊营养馕店的创始者。这家店在当地小有名气。

艾比班从小就喜欢吃馕，有一天，她跟母亲说："馕很美味，但是品种单一，为什么不加些核桃和牛奶？"于是，母亲就按照艾比班的方法做馕，发现这样做出来的馕好吃又有营养。于是，慢慢地，核桃馕、牛奶馕等都成了艾比班一家的创新产品。

营养	yíngyǎng	n.	nutrition; nourishment
馕	náng	n.	crusty pancake (staple food of the Uygur and Kazak ethnic groups)
创始者	chuàngshǐzhě	n.	founder; pioneer
小有名气	xiǎoyǒu-míngqì		have some reputation
美味	měiwèi	n.	fine food; table delicacies
单一	dānyī	adj.	single; unitary
核桃	hétao	n.	walnut

2009年，艾比班租下了第十五小学后面的一个十几平米的店铺。小店的货架上摆满了一家人的"试验品"，对外售卖。

2011年，艾比班的父亲注资馕店，但由于缺人手，又找不到足够大的门店，馕店的发展始终没有起色。直到2012年，艾比班将馕店搬到一个民俗文化手工业基地，馕店的发展才开始走上正轨。

店铺	diànpù	n.	shop; store
货架	huòjià	n.	goods shelf
试验品	shìyànpǐn	n.	experimental sample
售卖	shòumài	v.	sell
注资	zhùzī	v.	inject capital
人手	rénshǒu	n.	manpower; hand
起色	qǐsè	n.	improvement; pickup
民俗	mínsú	n.	folk custom
正轨	zhèngguǐ	n.	right track

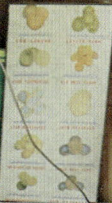

这个基地由江苏省南京市援建，约有48家商铺，所有商铺免租金五年。基地还帮助商户参加展销会，联系媒体记者采访，西帕伊营养馕店的名气逐渐大了起来。

店里的馕主要批发给飞机场、火车站和馕零售店铺，一般每天要用掉12袋25公斤的面粉，订单多的时候，要用掉15袋。

艾比班说，现在店里已经能接到一些来自北京、上海的订单了。

援建	yuánjiàn	v.	provide aid in construction
租金	zūjīn	n.	rent
展销会	zhǎnxiāohuì	n.	commodities fair
零售	língshòu	v.	retail; sell by retail
面粉	miànfěn	n.	(wheat) flour
订单	dìngdān	n.	purchase order

2015年，西帕伊营养馕店在墩买里开了六家分店，包括一家冰激凌店，一家奶茶店，四家馕零售店，总面积400平方米，员工45名。

　　艾比班说，平时上课工作压力很大，店铺由家人管理，周末或假期时她才有时间照看店铺。店铺能有今天的规模，是她最初不曾想到的。

墩买里	Dūnmǎilǐ	p.n.	name of a place
分店	fēndiàn	n.	branch (of a shop)
奶茶	nǎichá	n.	milk tea
压力	yālì	n.	pressure; stress
假期	jiàqī	n.	holiday; vacation; break
照看	zhàokàn	v.	attend to; look after

艾比班有一个十二岁的女儿和一个五岁的儿子，平时住在孩子奶奶家里。不忙的时候，她便来探望两个孩子。

维吾尔族人离不开馕，一天吃三顿都不会腻，但是很少有人知道馕的营养价值。

艾比班说，她想退休后开一家大型工厂，让学校的孩子去工厂实习，研制更多馕的品种，传播馕传统和馕文化，让更多人了解馕的医疗价值。

（本文选编自腾讯网《中国人的一天》栏目，作者：孟菁。）

腻	nì	adj.	bored of; fed up with
研制	yánzhì	v.	develop; prepare
医疗	yīliáo	n.	medical care

话说新疆馕

The Story of Xinjiang Naan

　　馕是新疆维吾尔自治区的主食之一，已经有两千多年的历史。在新疆，无论哪个季节，无论走到哪里，都可以吃到香香的馕。

　　馕品种丰富，常见的有肉馕、油馕、芝麻馕等。用羊肉丁、洋葱末等拌馅儿烤制的是肉馕，添加羊油的是油馕，将芝麻、葡萄汁等拌馅儿烤制的是芝麻馕。馕有许多形状，但大多是圆形，中间薄，边缘厚。最大的馕直径有40～50厘米，最小的馕只有茶杯口那么大，用来出远门携带。

　　在新疆，几乎家家都有烤馕的馕坑。馕坑一般都设在自家院子里，形状像一个大水缸。在馕坑外围，有专门供人站上去烤馕的方形土台。

　　馕的营养价值丰富，具有保养脾胃、杀菌、降血脂等作用。维吾尔族人的生活离不开馕，"可以一日无菜，但不可以一日无馕"。在招待客人时，主人往往也会拿出各种各样的馕。如果到库车县的维吾尔族人家中做客，他们会把最大的馕到最小的馕都摞起来，摆成塔形，放在桌子的中央，叫你饱尝。

在一些场合，馕还表达着特殊的含义。比如结婚时，新郎和新娘要抢着吃蘸了盐水的馕。因为维吾尔族人非常爱惜盐，馕也是他们生活中不可缺少的，把这两种珍贵的东西放在一起食用，象征着大家祝愿新郎、新娘如同盐和馕那样永不分离。

Naan is one of the major staple foods in Xinjiang Uygur Autonomous Region and has a history of more than two thousand years. In Xinjiang, whenever it is and wherever you go, you can always taste delicious naan.

Naan has a variety of types, and commonly seen ones are meat naan, oil naan and sesame naan, etc. Meat naan is baked with mixed fillings of diced mutton, chopped onions and other stuffing. Oil naan is baked with mutton fat. Sesame naan is baked with mixed fillings of sesame, grape juice, etc. Naan also has a variety of shapes, but is mainly baked in a round shape, with a thin centre and thick edges. The diameter of the largest naan may reach 40 to 50 centimetres, while the smallest naan may be only as large as a tea cup mouth, which is portable for long-distance travel.

In Xinjiang, almost every family has their own tandoor to bake naan. The naan tandoor is usually built in their own courtyards and is shaped like a giant water tank. There is a square earthen platform built surrounding the tandoor for people to stand on when baking naan.

Naan is nutritious, able to keep the spleen and stomach healthy and can kill bacteria and reduce blood lipid. Naan is an inseparable part of Uygur people's daily life, just as the local saying goes, "One can live a day without dishes yet cannot live a day without naan." Various naan will always be offered by hosts to treat guests. If you go to visit a Uygur family in Kuqa County, they will pile naan of all sizes up in

a tower shape and place them on the centre of a table so that you can gorge yourself.

On some occasions, naan also has special meanings. For instance, on wedding ceremonies, brides and bridegrooms will grab and eat naan that has been dipped in salt water. Uygur people cherish salt very much and naan is also an indivisible part of their life, so eating the two kinds of valuable food together symbolises their wishes for the newlyweds to be indivisible ever after, just like the salt and naan.

请上网查找并观看《舌尖上的中国》中关于新疆和田馕的介绍。

Please go online to find and watch a video clip of *A Bite of China* to learn about naan of Hotan City in Xinjiang.

Jìyì   zhōng de nián

记忆中的年

Spring Festival from Memory

对孩子而言，过年意味着新衣服、压岁钱和好吃好玩的；对大人而言，过年意味着一家人团团圆圆、热热闹闹。

Celebrating the Spring Festival means new clothes, lucky money, delicious food and all kinds of fun for children; while for grown-ups, the Spring Festival is a merry family reunion.

小时候，我一定是这个世界上最盼望**过年**的小孩之一。过年意味着放寒假回家，拥有一段较长时间的"自由"。

迄今为止，我只有三次没在潘庄过年，每一次，我都会无比想念在潘庄过年的情景。这些年，我试着用相机记录下潘庄过年的景象，捡拾一些记忆碎片，拼凑出我印象中潘庄过年的热闹气氛。

潘庄	Pānzhuāng	p.n.	name of a village
捡拾	jiǎnshí	v.	collect; gather
碎片	suìpiàn	n.	fragment; piece
拼凑	pīncòu	v.	put/piece together

● 过年 guònián

正月初一是中国的春节，这是中国最重要、最
热闹的传统节日。过年是指人们在春节期间进
行庆祝活动，包括吃团圆饭、贴春联、放鞭
炮、拜年等。

The Spring Festival falls on the first day of
the first Chinese lunar month. It is the most
important and joyful traditional festival in
China. People celebrate the New Year with a
series of activities, including having a family
reunion dinner, putting up the Spring Festival
couplets, setting off fireworks and visiting
relatives and friends, etc.

农历腊月二十五，宗岭哥想赶着在年前翻完地，为过完年种土豆做好准备。对于农耕来说，过年就是休息。年后农活儿再起，年也就结束了。

● 农历 nónglì
农历是中国传统历法，与农业生产有关，中国的传统节日一般按照农历日期进行庆祝，如端午节（农历五月初五）、中秋节（农历八月十五）等。

Chinese lunar calendar is a traditional calendric system related to agricultural activities. Traditional Chinese festivals are usually celebrated on certain days of the lunar calendar, such as the Dragon Boat Festival (the fifth day of the fifth lunar month), the Mid-Autumn Festival (the fifteenth day of the eighth lunar month), etc.

腊月	làyuè	n.	twelfth month of the lunar year
翻地	fāndì	v.	turn up the soil
农耕	nónggēng	n.	farming
农活儿	nónghuór	n.	farm work

腊月二十六下午，我和王四一起坐车回潘庄过年。就算爷爷奶奶知道我们会在哪一刻走进家门，他们见到我们的第一句话也是"哎呀，你们怎么回来了？"我们回家过年了呀！

　　下车时，我们惊奇地发现，村里已经装上了路灯。王四提着行李大步前行，向走在后面的我喊道："变化真大，都不敢认了！"

就算	jiùsuàn	*conj.*	even if
路灯	lùdēng	*n.*	streetlight; street/road lamp
行李	xíngli	*n.*	luggage; baggage
前行	qiánxíng	*v.*	go/move forward

腊月二十七是镇上这一年的最后一个集，也就是年集。这是一年之中规模最大、最热闹的集。大家都愿意起个大早，到年集上遛一圈。十四五岁的半大孩子喜欢结伴而去，稍小一些的孩子们则会跟着父母一起去。这时，孩子们如果向大人讨买自己喜欢的东西，一般都会得到满足。

集	jí	n.	country fair; market
遛	liù	v.	walk leisurely; stroll
半大	bàndà	n.	age between adulthood and childhood
结伴	jiébàn	v.	go with
讨	tǎo	v.	ask/beg for

鱼是潘庄过年的必备食材，祭祀的供桌
上少不了鱼的影子，"年年有余"这个成语
已经解释了一切。腊月二十八，奶奶弄好了
过年吃的鱼，晾在板上。

● **年年有余** niánnián-yǒuyú
中国传统祈福的吉祥话，"鱼"和
"余"同音，过年吃鱼寄托了人们希
望来年生活富足，拥有多余的粮食和财
富的美好心愿。
It is a traditional Chinese saying for blessings. In Chinese,
the pronunciation of the character "鱼" (fish) is the same
as that of "余" (affluence). So by eating fish on the Spring
Festival, people wish for a bountiful year ahead with
plenty of food and fortune.

必备	bìbèi	v.	be essential to/for
食材	shícái	n.	ingredient; food
祭祀	jìsì	v.	offer sacrifices to gods/ancestors
供桌	gòngzhuō	n.	altar table

腊月二十九，除夕前一天，我的爷爷和奶奶在打扫屋子准备过年。墙上的影视明星挂历和年画已经贴了近三十年了。奖状是我小学时的"荣誉"，也贴了十多年了。

除夕	chúxī	n.	New Year's Eve
影视	yǐngshì	n.	film and television
挂历	guàlì	n.	wall calendar
年画	niánhuà	n.	Spring Festival picture
奖状	jiǎngzhuàng	n.	certificate of merit/award

　　除夕下午，村民顾成军和回家过年的大儿子一起在客厅里包饺子。他的老婆在厨房里准备晚上祭祀的供品。

村民	cūnmín	n.	villager
饺子	jiǎozi	n.	*jiaozi*; Chinese dumpling
供品	gòngpǐn	n.	offering

除夕夜晚，胆小的王子佳躲在门后看堂哥在院子里放鞭炮。

胆小	dǎnxiǎo	adj.	timid; cowardly
堂哥	tánggē	n.	cousin
放鞭炮	fàng biānpào		set off firecrackers

除夕夜，当老伴儿和儿子、儿媳在包饺子时，刘大爷正入神地看着中央电视台春节联欢晚会，他的两个孙子则趴在床边看电影。刘大爷的两个儿子都生活在城里，平时只有他和老伴儿带着一个孙子生活在潘庄。为了解决孩子们回家房间不够用的问题，刘大爷盖了这间十多平米的厨房，平时做饭，也能住人。他的二儿子买了一台50寸的液晶彩电放在客厅，老彩电就放在厨房了。

老伴儿	lǎobànr	n.	(of an old couple) husband or wife
儿媳	érxí	n.	daughter-in-law
大爷	dàye	n.	uncle (a respectful form of address for an elderly man)
入神	rùshén	v.	be entranced
趴	pā	v.	lie on one's stomach
寸	cùn	m.	*cun* (a unit of length, equal to 1/3 decimetre)
液晶彩电	yèjīng cǎidiàn		liquid crystal TV

● **春节联欢晚会**

Chūnjié Liánhuān Wǎnhuì

春节联欢晚会是中国中央电视台在每年农历除夕晚上为庆祝春节举办的综艺性文艺晚会。节目时间从除夕晚上八点持续到午夜，大约4.5个小时。

The Spring Festival Gala is a CCTV variety show aired on the New Year's Eve to celebrate the Spring Festival. The show lasts four and a half hours, starting from 20:00 till past the midnight.

到了凌晨，潘庄村开始动起来了。每个家庭都沉浸在急促的炸裂声中。烟花在潘庄并不多见，在只有三百多户人家的潘庄，谁家院子里放烟花，附近人家就都能看到。

沉浸	chénjìn	v.	be immersed (in sth)
急促	jícù	adj.	hurried; rapid
炸裂	zhàliè	v.	explode; blow up
烟花	yānhuā	n.	fireworks
人家	rénjiā	n.	household

大年初一的潘庄，满是串门儿拜年的人群。人们早早地起床，清扫前夜散落在院子里的鞭炮残屑，在屋里放好凳子，摆好赶集买来的糖果和瓜子儿，打开迎宾的大门。

串门儿	chuànménr	v.	drop in on sb
拜年	bàinián	v.	pay a New Year visit
清扫	qīngsǎo	v.	thoroughly clean up
散落	sànluò	v.	fall scattered
残屑	cánxiè	n.	scrap
瓜子儿	guāzǐr	n.	melon seed
迎宾	yíngbīn	v.	greet/welcome guests

初一上午，老人们在家里等着客人来访，年轻人则出门去拜年。拜年的人们大多结伴而行。男人、女人、孩子都有各自的队伍，不是一帮近亲，就是一群好友，特别是在外回乡的人们，正好同行叙旧。串门儿的人们在胡同里碰到了会相互打招呼。

送走了一拨串门儿的乡邻，振冉奶奶赶紧开始擦拭桌子，准备迎接新一拨客人。

来访	**láifǎng**	*v.*	come to visit	拨	**bō**	*m.*	group; team
帮	**bāng**	*m.*	group; band	乡邻	**xiānglín**	*n.*	fellow villager
近亲	**jìnqīn**	*n.*	close relative	振冉	**Zhènrǎn**	*p.n.*	name of a person
叙旧	**xùjiù**	*v.*	talk about the past	擦拭	**cāshì**	*v.*	clean; wipe

在潘庄，过了大年初一就要忙着走亲戚。

农历正月初二，绪茂大爷和另一位村民坐在路边闲谈。一辆来潘庄走亲戚的红色小轿车停在他们背后，而轿车的主人此时正在接受招待。

过年既闲又忙，闲在没有农活儿，忙在走亲访友。

● **走亲戚** zǒu qīnqi
走亲戚是指春节时拜访亲戚的活动。传统的走亲戚从正月初二可以一直持续到正月十六，走亲戚时一般都会带上礼品，离开时主人也会回赠礼物。

It refers to the custom of visiting relatives during the Spring Festival. Traditionally, people start visiting relatives from the second day of the first lunar month till the sixteenth day. It is customary to bring gifts to relatives and receive gifts in return while leaving.

正月	**zhēngyuè**	*n.*	first month of the lunar year
闲谈	**xiántán**	*v.*	chat
轿车	**jiàochē**	*n.*	car
走亲访友	**zǒuqīn-fǎngyǒu**		visit one's relatives and friends

农历正月初三，一户村民给城里来走亲戚的客人抬上三袋白菜。潘庄村民总要给来走亲戚的客人回赠点儿什么，或者请客人带回部分礼品。所以，在年后的潘庄，经常可以看到村民和要离开的亲友在家门口"推搡"——亲友不愿意带礼物回去，主人家却一定要给。

白菜	báicài	n.	Chinese cabbage
回赠	huízèng	v.	give sb a gift in return
礼品	lǐpǐn	n.	present; gift
推搡	tuīsǎng	v.	push; decline

等到正月初五、初六，亲戚都走动得差不多了，人们开始走访朋友。每到这个时候，我的爷爷奶奶就会张罗一桌酒席，让父亲和我去请邻居来家里做客。我们平时不在身边，年老的他们离不开邻居的帮助。

晚上送这些邻居离开时，我们的寒暄告别总会引来狗叫，它们已经从爆竹声的惊吓中缓过神来了。

我知道，年已经过完了。

（本文选编自腾讯网《中国人的一天》栏目，

作者： 刘磊。）

走动	zǒudòng	v.	(of relatives and friends) visit each other
张罗	zhāngluo	v.	plan and prepare
酒席	jiǔxí	n.	feast; banquet
做客	zuòkè	v.	be a guest/visitor
寒暄	hánxuān	v.	exchange (conventional) greetings
垃圾	lājī	n.	rubbish; garbage

过完年，潘庄村的垃圾集中箱已经盛满。

"恭喜发财，红包拿来！"

"May You Be Prosperous, and Red Envelopes Please!"

　　"恭喜发财，红包拿来！"这是中国人过年时常说的一句俏皮的吉祥话。将崭新的人民币用红纸包起来，作为压岁钱分发给晚辈，是中国人庆祝春节的传统习俗。红色象征着活力、愉快和好运，红包寄托的是长辈对晚辈的美好祝愿。因为"压岁"与"压祟"谐音，所以压岁钱代表压住邪祟，平平安安。

　　挨家挨户拜年是许多人儿时的记忆，而小孩子最盼望的莫过于收红包了。如今，随着互联网的兴起，人们庆祝春节的形式发生了变化，红包也进入了"数字时代"。过年期间，用微信、QQ、支付宝等发红包，已经成为亿万中国人与亲朋好友分享快乐的新方式。

　　但是，人们对电子红包的态度却不尽相同。有人认为，微信可以将红包同时发给一群朋友，让应用程序决定每个人"抢"到多少钱，就像玩游戏一样。他们觉得使用这种方式发送节日祝福比传统红包方便多了。另一些人却觉得，收发电子红包使得很多年轻人没有和家人好好交流，也不再参与包饺子、看春晚等活动。

　　不管是越来越流行的电子红包，还是传统的红包，都会是春节最受大家欢迎的礼物。过年的方式在与时俱进，但阖家团聚、祈求幸福是中国人过年永远不变的主题。

"May you be prosperous, and red envelopes please!" are playful auspicious words often heard during the Chinese New Year. It is a tradition for Chinese people to celebrate the Spring Festival by wrapping brand-new banknotes with red paper and giving them to younger generations as lucky money. Red symbolises vitality, delight and good fortune, and red envelopes convey good wishes from the elders to the younger generation. The pronunciation of "yasui" in Chinese sounds exactly like "suppressing the evil". Therefore, lucky money symbolises keeping off evil spirits and being safe and sound.

Going from door to door wishing people a Happy New Year is in many people's childhood memories, and what children yearn for the most is definitely receiving red envelopes. Nowadays, with the rise of the Internet, people are changing their ways of celebrating the Spring Festival and red envelopes are also entering the "digital age". During the Chinese New Year, sending out electronic red envelopes via WeChat, QQ, Alipay, etc has become a fashion for hundreds of millions of Chinese to share joy and happiness with their family and friends.

However, people have different opinions toward the electronic red envelopes. Some people take it as a game of sending electronic red envelopes to a bunch of friends and letting the application system decide the amount of money everyone gets. They think it is much more convenient than sending out holiday wishes by giving out traditional red envelopes. Others think that electronic red envelopes have prevented many young people from having quality conversations with their family. And they no longer participate in activities such as making dumplings and watching the Spring Festival Gala.

Be it the increasingly popular electronic red envelopes or the traditional red envelopes, both are the most popular gifts during the Spring Festival. As the ways of celebrating the Chinese New Year evolve with the times, the theme of family reunion and prayers for happiness remains eternal for Chinese people.

文化链接 Cultural Links

中国人过年时有丰富多彩的传统习俗，这些习俗都寄托了人们辞旧迎新的美好愿望。请把下面这些习俗和对应的寓意连起来。

Chinese New Year is celebrated with a variety of colourful traditional customs, each symbolising people's hopes for bidding farewell to the old and welcoming the new. Please connect the following customs with their corresponding meanings.

大扫除 ·
spring cleaning

吃年糕 ·
eating New Year cakes

发压岁钱 ·
giving red envelopes

全家一起吃饺子 ·
family gathering to eat *jiaozi*

贴对联，放鞭炮 ·
posting Spring Festival couplets
and setting off firecrackers

除夕夜守岁 ·
staying up late on New Year's Eve

· 驱逐"年兽"，祈求平安
expelling the "年" monster, praying for peace

· 家庭团聚，幸福美满
family reunion, happiness and harmony

· 年年高升，一年更比一年好
rising year by year, each year better than the last

· 扫除"陈旧"，迎接新春
sweeping away the old, welcoming the spring

· 珍惜时间，希望父母长命百岁
treasuring time, wishing for longevity of parents

· 压"祟"驱邪，平安过年
driving away evil spirits, celebrating a safe New Year

"Yǐngchī"　Liú　lǎoshī
"影痴" 刘老师
Mr Liu: A Teacher and Devoted Cineaste

　　刘燚，大连理工大学硕士研究生毕业，现在是沈阳一所大学的教师，电影爱好者。人生的角色重在演好自己的剧情，而他却想当人生的导演。

Liu Yi, graduated from Dalian University of Technology with a master's degree, is now a university teacher in Shenyang and a devoted cineaste. One's lifetime role is to play well one's own story, and Liu wants to be a director of his life.

人生最好的角色，就是演好属于自己的剧情，而一位80后大学教师，却想当自己人生的导演，在自己设计的剧情里自由穿行。他叫刘燚，硕士毕业于大连理工大学，现在在沈阳一所大学当老师。作为一名资深电影爱好者，他看了近万部电影。早年在英国短暂留学期间，他还观看了近百部英文舞台剧。

剧情	jùqíng	n.	plot of a play/an opera
80后	80 hòu	n.	the post-1980s
穿行	chuānxíng	v.	pass/go through
刘燚	Liú Yì	p.n.	name of a person
短暂	duǎnzàn	adj.	of short duration
舞台剧	wǔtáijù	n.	stage play

微电影	**wēidiànyǐng**	*n.*	short film
萌芽	**méngyá**	*v.*	bud; germinate
录像机	**lùxiàngjī**	*n.*	video recorder
积攒	**jīzǎn**	*v.*	collect/save bit by bit

2012年，刘燚在工作之余开始写微电影剧本，还得了奖。

刘燚的电影梦在他小时候就萌芽了。七岁时，他开始喜欢看电影，家里的一台录像机是他的宝贝。上大学以后，他基本每天都看电影，而电影背后的那个"角色"就成了他追求的梦想。刘燚的家里积攒了许多世界经典电影的光盘。

刘燚在大学时就开始写剧本，至今已经撰写微电影剧本20多部，其中10部已经拍摄，而且几乎全部获过奖。有了专业评委的首肯，他更加坚定自己的梦想了。刘燚的工资收入并不高，但他还是攒了两年，花了几万元添置了昂贵的录影设备。

撰写	zhuànxiě	v.	write (usually short articles)
拍摄	pāishè	v.	shoot; photograph
评委	píngwěi	n.	member of a review committee; judge
首肯	shǒukěn	v.	approve
添置	tiānzhì	v.	add to one's possessions
录影	lùyǐng	v.	videotape; record

　　2013年，他兼任制片、编剧、导演、演员等职的作品《夜路》参赛，并获得微电影大赛优秀作品奖，从此他便开始踏上了属于自己的影视制作道路。今年，在辽宁首届微电影大赛中，同样由他任制片、编剧、导演、演员等职的《苹果》获得了最高奖项。

兼任	jiānrèn	v.	hold a concurrent post
制片	zhìpiàn	n.	producer; film maker
编剧	biānjù	n.	playwright
职	zhí	n.	post; office
奖项	jiǎngxiàng	n.	prize

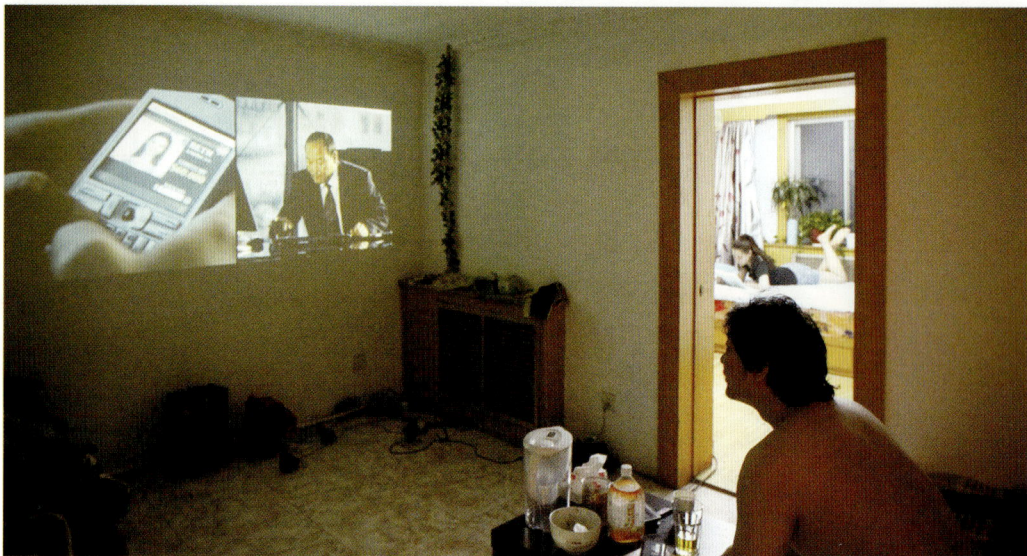

　　平时，除了正常上班讲课，刘燚满脑子想的都是剧情。多数情况下，家里客厅墙壁上投射的电影，是他每天晚饭后的忠实"朋友"。他也常常因此忽略了刚结婚四年的妻子。不过，妻子非常支持他。为了不影响妻子休息，刘燚在卧室门外摆了一张简易床，有时看电影太晚就睡在卧室外面。

墙壁	**qiángbì**	*n.*	wall
投射	**tóushè**	*v.*	project; cast
简易	**jiǎnyì**	*adj.*	simply equipped

因为过于忙碌，结婚四年多了，他还没要孩子。然而，他又非常喜欢孩子，每当电影里有父亲的角色时，他都主动要求扮演。

　　2014年10月，刘嫩做了一档点评院线电影的网络视频节目《院线风向标》，每周一期，评论和推荐最新上映的院线电影。

　　因为没有固定的演播室，刘嫩就到一些热爱电影的朋友的公司或家里，录制他的影评视频。刘嫩是个多面手，《院线风向标》的采集、编辑、播放都由他自己完成。

档	dàng	m.	(used for events, etc)
点评	diǎnpíng	v.	comment
院线	yuànxiàn	n.	theatre chain; cinema
风向标	fēngxiàngbiāo	n.	weathercock
上映	shàngyìng	v.	release; show (a film)
演播室	yǎnbōshì	n.	studio
录制	lùzhì	v.	record; video
影评	yǐngpíng	n.	film review
多面手	duōmiànshǒu	n.	jack-of-all-trades; versatile person

有时，刘燚在外拍电影要到后半夜才能结束，但他从没因此耽误过正常的工作和教学。

在一次电影拍摄中，刘燚不小心崴伤了脚，他就这样在半个月里一瘸一拐地去给学生上课。

刘燚工作认真，讲课幽默有趣。在他的课堂上，经常能听见一阵阵笑声。

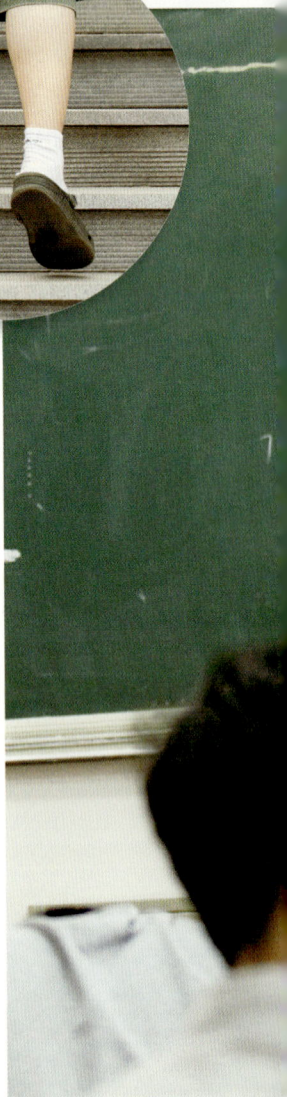

后半夜	hòubànyè	n.	after midnight
崴	wǎi	v.	sprain; twist
一瘸一拐	yìqué-yìguǎi		walk with a limp
课堂	kètáng	n.	classroom

在业余时间或周末，刘燚经常参加一些电影讲座和论坛，在沈阳电影圈里小有名气。

为了节约开支，刘燚常去联系一些免费拍电影的场地。几年下来，他的足迹几乎遍布沈阳的各个角落。目前，刘燚正在筹备自己的第一部网络大电影，打算今年开机。同时，他也在构思自己的第一个院线电影剧本。

（本文选编自腾讯网《中国人的一天》栏目，作者：吴章杰。）

圈	quān	n.	circle
场地	chǎngdì	n.	space; place
足迹	zújì	n.	footprint; track
开机	kāijī	v.	(of a film, etc) start shooting

华语电影三大奖

Three Major Awards of Chinese Film

金鸡奖、金像奖、金马奖一起被称为华语电影三大奖。

金鸡奖是中国大陆电影界最权威、最专业的电影奖，创立于 1981 年，因当年是中国农历鸡年而得名。金鸡奖由数十位专业评审组成评审团，集中看片投票决定获奖者，所以又被称为"专家奖"。金鸡奖的奖杯是一只伸着脖子的金鸡，意思是以金鸡啼晓鼓励电影工作者闻鸡起舞。金鸡奖设有 20 个左右奖项，每两年评选一次。

金像奖创立于 1982 年。金像奖的评审制度与奥斯卡金像奖类似，是由电影人全面主导和参与的电影奖项。金像奖的奖杯是一个手持星球、身围胶片、姿态积极、充满向往感的女神造型，奖杯名叫"星光荣耀"。每年的金像奖颁奖是中国香港电影界年度最重要的活动，一般在 4 月中旬举行，设有 20 余个奖项。

创立于 1962 年的金马奖是中国台湾地区主办的电影奖项，每年举

办一届。金马奖的评选面向所有华语电影和华语电影人，它是华语电影圈中历史最悠久的奖项。金马奖的奖杯是一匹意气风发、腾空跃起的马。

　　这三大电影奖对华语电影的发展都起着巨大的推动作用，多年来奖励了许多优秀的电影作品和电影工作者。演员周迅和章子怡都曾经凭借自己在电影作品中的出色表演，先后获得过这三项大奖的最佳女主角。

The three major awards for Chinese-language films are the Golden Rooster Awards, the Hong Kong Film Awards and the Golden Horse Awards.

The Golden Rooster Awards are the most professional film awards with the highest authority in China's mainland. The name of the awards came from the Year of the Rooster in 1981 when the awards were set up. The award recipients are selected and voted for by a jury consisting of dozens of film experts who view the films collectively. That is why the awards are also called the "expert awards". The award statuette is a golden rooster stretching its neck, which signifies encouraging film workers to rise up and practise swordsmanship upon hearing the crow of a rooster. The awards include around 20 award categories, and the ceremony is held every two years.

The Hong Kong Film Awards were founded in 1982. Its review system is similar to that of the Oscars, fully led and participated by people of the film circles. Its statuette, called "Starlight Glory", is an enthusiastic and aspiring goddess holding a globe in her hands while wrapped by rolls of film. The annual

award ceremony is the most significant event in China's Hong Kong film circle. Generally, it is held in mid-April, with more than 20 award categories presented.

The Golden Horse Awards, founded in 1962, are held annually in Taiwan, China. The awards are open to all Chinese-language films and Chinese film-makers, and have the longest history in Chinese-language film circle. The award statuette is a high-spirited and vigorous horse jumping into the air.

The three major awards have contributed enormously to the development of Chinese-language films, and also have rewarded brilliant films and encouraged talented film workers over the years. Zhou Xun and Zhang Ziyi were both awarded for their outstanding performances in the films as the best actresses respectively by the three awards.

文化链接 Cultural Links

你喜欢看电影吗？你最喜欢的演员或导演是谁？请填写下表，并给同伴介绍一下。

Do you enjoy watching films? Who is your favourite actor/actress or director? Please fill in the form below and introduce him/her to your peers.

我最喜欢的演员/导演 My Favourite Actor/Actress or Director	
姓名 name	
国籍 nationality	
出生日期 date of birth	
职业 occupation	
代表作品 representative works	
我喜欢他/她的理由 the reason why I like him/her	

"Hóngxiù Xuānzhǔ"

"红绣轩主"

"Master of the Red Embroidery Chamber"

杨小婷是湖北省工艺美术大师，中国非物质文化遗产汉绣的带头人之一。她给自己的住所取名"红绣轩"，自号"红绣轩主"。

Yang Xiaoting, a master of arts and crafts in Hubei Province, is one of the leading experts of China's intangible cultural heritage Han embroidery. She named her own residence the "Red Embroidery Chamber", and called herself "Master of the Red Embroidery Chamber".

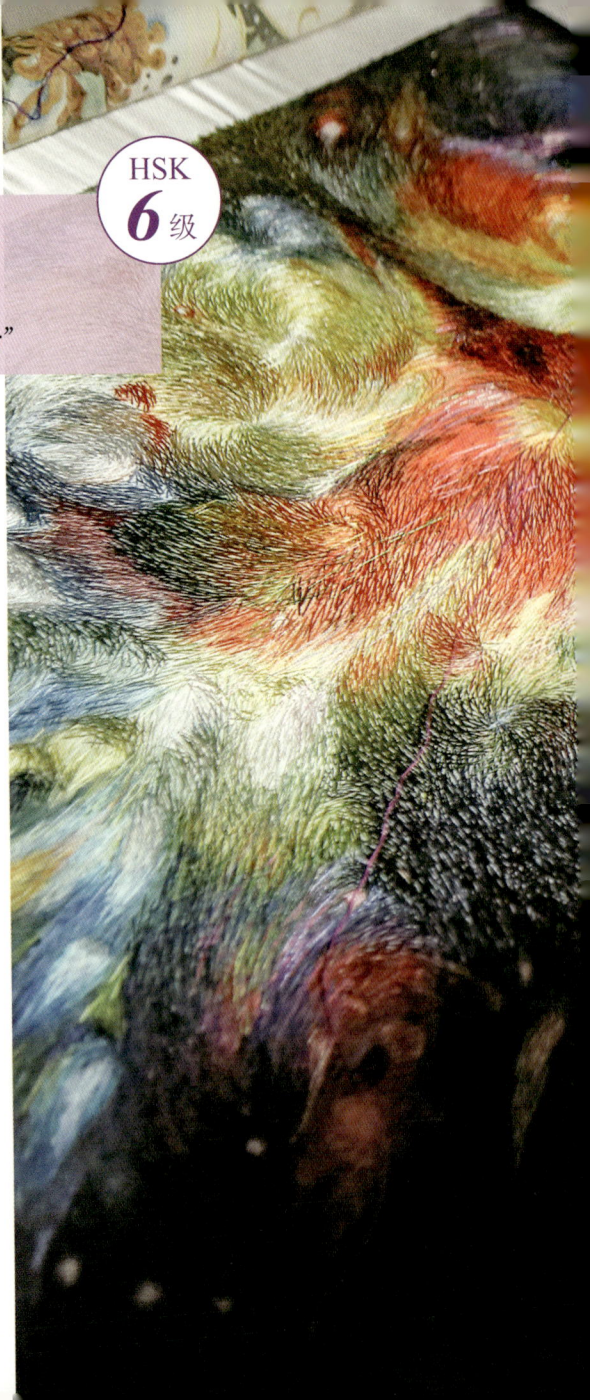

杨小婷，湖北省工艺美术大师，中国非物质文化遗产项目汉绣的带头人之一。今年只有35岁的她就像是一位从民国电视剧中走出来的人物。

她给自己的住所取名"红绣轩"，自号"红绣轩主"。

大师	dàshī	*n.*	grand master (used to address scholar/expert of outstanding achievements)
带头人	dàitóurén	*n.*	leader
民国	Mínguó	*p.n.*	Republic of China (1912~1949)
住所	zhùsuǒ	*n.*	dwelling place; residence
轩	xuān	*n.*	small room or veranda with windows (used in names of studios, restaurants or teahouses in ancient times)

汉绣主要流行于湖北地区，曾多次在北京展出，还参加过国际展览，并受到好评。虽然汉绣在中国的知名度不如"四大名绣"，但在杨小婷眼中，这些并不是问题，因为汉绣在2011年迎来了一个发展契机——杨小婷汉绣研究基地在昙华林落户。她有信心带出一批优秀的汉绣大师，推动汉绣的发展。

● 四大名绣　sì dà míngxiù
在中国传统刺绣工艺品当中，常常将江苏的苏绣、湖南的湘绣、广东的粤绣和四川的蜀绣合称为中国"四大名绣"。
The four major styles of traditional Chinese embroidery usually refer to Su embroidery from Jiangsu Province, Xiang embroidery from Hunan Province, Yue embroidery from Guangdong Province and Shu embroidery from Sichuan Province.

好评	hǎopíng	n.	favourable comment; good review
知名度	zhīmíngdù	n.	popularity
契机	qìjī	n.	turning point; juncture
昙华林	Tánhuálín	p.n.	name of a place
落户	luòhù	v.	settle (down)

● 龙袍 lóngpáo

龙袍是指古代帝王穿的袍服，因袍上绣有龙形图案而得名。皇帝的龙袍一般绣有九条龙。

The dragon robe is the robe for ancient Chinese emperors. Its name came from the dragon patterns embroidered on the robe. Typically, there are nine dragons on an emperor's dragon robe.

杨小婷在昙华林公开招徒，目前昙华林的六家绣坊均由她的高徒创办。与人们印象中的那些"福"字、"龙袍"不同，杨小婷的汉绣往往天马行空，充满生机。她说，汉绣是有美好未来的。

招徒	zhāotú	v.	recruit apprentice
绣坊	xiùfáng	n.	embroidery workshop
高徒	gāotú	n.	outstanding disciple
天马行空	tiānmǎ-xíngkōng		like a heavenly steed soaring across the skies— (of writing, calligraphy, etc) powerful and unconstrained in style
美好	měihǎo	adj.	(of life, future, wish, etc) fine; glorious

杨小婷说，她花了六年的时间，复活了汉绣已经失传的针法"游针绣"。这种针法也是汉绣区别于"四大名绣"的地方之一。凭借着自己深厚的油画功底，杨小婷创作的游针绣作品跟画儿一样传神。

这是杨小婷在创作一组名为《炫》的主题作品。她说《炫》这组作品由一大六小组成，希望问世时能够让人大吃一惊。

失传	shīchuán	v.	be lost; no longer exist
针法	zhēnfǎ	n.	stitch
游针绣	yóuzhēnxiù	n.	a way of needling
凭借	píngjiè	v.	rely on; depend on
深厚	shēnhòu	adj.	solid; deep-seated
油画	yóuhuà	n.	oil painting
功底	gōngdǐ	n.	basic training; foundation
传神	chuánshén	adj.	vivid; lifelike
问世	wènshì	v.	come out
大吃一惊	dàchīyìjīng		be greatly surprised

然而从2013年开始，攻击杨小婷的声音不断出现："昙华林没有真正的汉绣"，"杨小婷做的那不是汉绣"。汉绣出现内斗，不同风格涌现，都称自己为"正统"。

　　"很多人来质疑我，或者来向我讨说法，"杨小婷说，"开始我会解释，但后来我就不说什么了。汉绣的针法、技巧和特点有专家、学者和史料可以证明。"

内斗	nèidòu	v.	internal conflict
正统	zhèngtǒng	n.	legitimism
质疑	zhìyí	v.	call in question; query
讨说法	tǎo shuōfa		demand an explanation
学者	xuézhě	n.	scholar
史料	shǐliào	n.	historical data/materials

此前在网上有个帖子，称在昙华林看不到真正的汉绣。对此，杨小婷做出了这样的解释：一个大师一年只能出一两幅高端汉绣作品，所以价格很高，一般在几万到十几万之间。而昙华林是向外界展示汉绣的一个窗口，为了节省时间，很多作品会用先渲染再针织的方法，也有部分是批量生产的工艺品，价格只要百元上下，因此作品水平参差不齐。

帖子	tiězi	n.	posting
高端	gāoduān	n.	high-end
窗口	chuāngkǒu	n.	channel; show window
渲染	xuànrǎn	v.	apply colours to a drawing
针织	zhēnzhī	v.	knit
批量	pīliàng	adv.	in batches/bulk
参差不齐	cēncī-bùqí		uneven; varying

面对质疑，杨小婷"退隐"了。她说自己需要从第一线退下来，做点儿扎实的事情，专心培养人才，让汉绣市场减少一些混乱。

这已经是她个人的第二次"退隐"了。第一次她闭门近十年，复活了游针绣，出山时几幅作品震惊绣界；这一次，她说："我不会去争，历史自有评判。"

退隐	tuìyǐn	v.	(of an official) retire from public life
第一线	dì-yī xiàn	n.	forefront; frontline
闭门	bìmén	v.	close the door
出山	chūshān	v.	take up an official post
评判	píngpàn	v.	judge; determine

现在，杨小婷关了研究室，只留下一间办公室。她原本一周要去好几次昙华林，现在只是偶尔去进行一些指导。杨小婷的汉绣团队精英们热衷于汉绣，不为金钱。

杨小婷说："这样的人才能做好汉绣。我做的所有作品，卖出去的钱全部用于慈善，我没有通过卖作品获得一分钱，很多人不了解我的生活状态。"

原本	yuánběn	adv.	originally; formerly
精英	jīngyīng	n.	elite
热衷	rèzhōng	v.	be keen on; have a burning passion for
金钱	jīnqián	n.	money

杨小婷说："艺术都是随着时代发展的，汉绣也不应该只是历史某一个时期的那种风格，汉绣不会停滞不前。"

杨小婷每天都在自己的"红绣轩"中创作。晚上8点到12点，是杨小婷的工作时间。她说自己非常享受现在的状态，每天自然醒，白天几乎不出门，晚上则专注于创作。

| 停滞不前 | tíngzhì-bùqián | | remain stagnant |
| 专注 | zhuānzhù | v. | be concentrated |

杨小婷的研究室里摆满了个人作品和各色绣线。

绣线　　**xiùxiàn**　　*n.*　　thread

除了创作，杨小婷每天还会弹弹古琴或者钢琴，偶尔画画油画，整理一下院子。

● 古琴 gǔqín

古琴是中国传统弹拨乐器，至今已有3000多年历史，被中国古代文人视为高雅的象征。

Guqin is a traditional Chinese plucked string instrument with a history of over 3,000 years. It was viewed by the ancient Chinese scholars as a symbol of great elegance and refinement.

弹	tán	v.	play (a musical instrument)
钢琴	gāngqín	n.	piano
院子	yuànzi	n.	courtyard

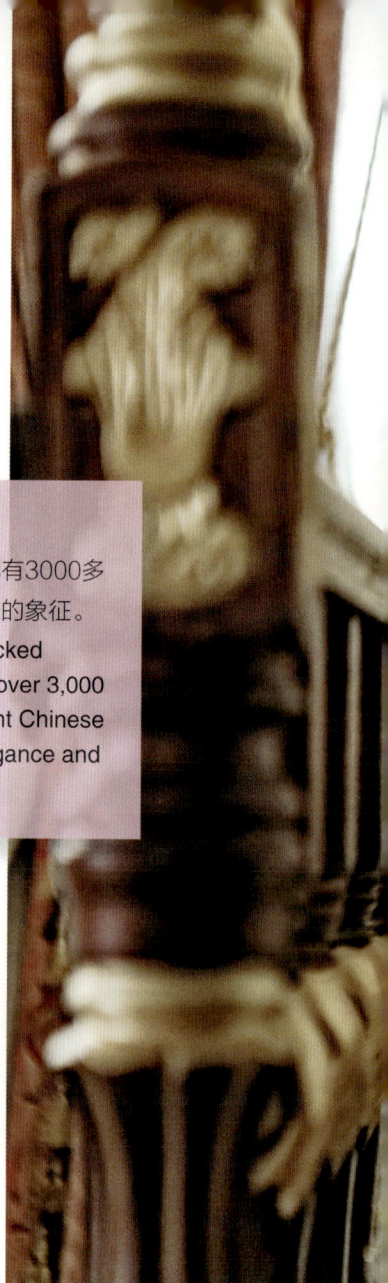

她还是个十足的服装和帽子控，家中有几百顶帽子，只要出门，一定会戴帽子。

这样的生活要过多久，杨小婷没有给出一个明确的回答。"但当我回来的时候，一定是汉绣繁荣到来的时候。"杨小婷自信地说。

（本文选编自腾讯网《中国人的一天》栏目，

作者：马路遥。）

十足	shízú	*adj.*	sheer; downright
明确	míngquè	*adj.*	clear and definite
繁荣	fánróng	*adj.*	flourishing; prosperous

~ 控 ~ kòng

网络用语，源于英文单词"complex"（情结）的前缀"com"，指痴迷于某人或某物的人。

Kong is an Internet buzzword that comes from the prefix "com" of the word "complex", referring to people who are obsessed with someone or something.

中国的刺绣

Chinese Embroidery

苏绣

刺绣是用针引线在绸缎或布帛上穿绕，形成各种图案的一种装饰方法。它是中国著名的传统手工艺品，迄今已有3000多年的历史。特色鲜明的苏绣、湘绣、粤绣和蜀绣被称为中国"四大名绣"。

苏绣发源于江苏苏州，已经有2000多年的历史。苏绣以绣工精细著称，艺人们可以把一根头发粗细的绣花线分成两根、四根以至十二根、四十八根细线绣，并将千万个线头、线结藏得无影无踪。无论从正面还是反面看，作品都栩栩如生。

湘绣是湖南出产的刺绣。湘绣多以中国画为蓝本，色彩丰富，风格豪放，形态生动逼真。典型的湘绣题材包括狮子、老虎等。

粤绣是广东地区的刺绣。其特点是色彩艳丽，图

湘绣

案整齐，题材多以龙、凤为主。与其他刺绣绣工一般为女子不同，粤绣绣工多为男子。

蜀绣出产在四川。蜀绣构图简练，用针工整，花纹边缘如同刀切一般齐整。蜀绣的针法有1000多种，题材多为花鸟、走兽、山水等。

除了"四大名绣"外，北京的京绣、温州的瓯绣、苗族的苗绣等地方刺绣也很有特色。刺绣既可以是供人们欣赏的艺术品，也可以用于服装、被面、枕套等生活用品，广受大家喜爱。

粤绣

Embroidery is to decorate silk or fabric by using needles and threads to stitch various patterns. It is a renowned traditional Chinese handicraft and has more than 3,000 years of history. The distinctive Su embroidery, Xiang embroidery, Yue embroidery and Shu embroidery are known as the four major styles of Chinese embroidery.

Originated in Suzhou, Jiangsu Province, Su embroidery has a history of over 2,000 years. It is famous for its meticulously skillful stitching. Su embroidery artists can split a thread as fine as a human hair into two, four, twelve or even forty-eight threads, and the ends and knots of tens of millions of threads are woven inside the silk, so the embroidered patterns on both sides are lifelike.

Xiang embroidery comes from Hunan Province. Usually based on Chinese paintings, Xiang embroidery presents richly coloured designs, bold and unconstrained styles and vivid and lifelike patterns. Typical themes of Xiang embroidery include lions and tigers, etc.

Yue embroidery is crafted in Guangdong Province. It features vibrant colours and symmetrical patterns. The themes of Yue embroidery are mostly dragons and phoenixes. Unlike other embroideries whose artists are usually women, Yue embroidery artists are mostly men.

Shu embroidery comes from Sichuan Province. It has simple compositions and neat stitches. The pattern edges are as neat as knife cuts. Shu embroidery has over 1,000 kinds of stitch, and its most common themes are flowers, birds, animals, landscapes and so on.

In addition to the four major embroideries, Jing embroidery from Beijing, Ou embroidery from Wenzhou, Miao embroidery of the Miao ethnic group are also distinguished regional embroideries. Embroidery is not only a work of art for people to admire but also can be used to decorate clothing, quilt covers, pillowcases and other daily necessities, so it is widely loved.

　　旗袍是中国女性的传统服装，上面有各种美丽的刺绣图案。请你发挥想象，给这件旗袍设计一些刺绣图案吧！

　　Mandarin gown is a traditional Chinese dress for women. It has a variety of beautiful embroidery patterns. Please try to design some embroidery patterns for this mandarin gown with imagination.

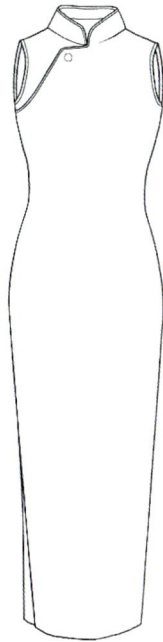

词汇索引

词语	拼音	词性	含义	页码
串门儿	chuànménr	*v.*	drop in on sb	80
创可贴	chuāngkětiē	*n.*	Band-Aid	25
窗口	chuāngkǒu	*n.*	channel; show window	127
创始者	chuàngshǐzhě	*n.*	founder; pioneer	49
村民	cūnmín	*n.*	villager	74
寸	cùn	*m.*	*cun* (a unit of length, equal to 1/3 decimetre)	76
大吃一惊	dàchīyìjīng		be greatly surprised	123
大人	dàren	*n.*	adult; grown-up	6
大师	dàshī	*n.*	grand master (used to address scholar/expert of outstanding achievements)	117
大爷	dàye	*n.*	uncle (a respectful form of address for an elderly man)	76
带头人	dàitóurén	*n.*	leader	117
单一	dānyī	*adj.*	single; unitary	49
胆小	dǎnxiǎo	*adj.*	timid; cowardly	75
当中	dāngzhōng	*n.*	centre; middle	34
档	dàng	*m.*	(used for events, etc)	105
第一线	dì-yī xiàn	*n.*	forefront; frontline	128
点评	diǎnpíng	*v.*	comment	105
电动车	diàndòngchē	*n.*	electric vehicle	29
电商	diànshāng	*n.*	e-business; e-commerce	23
店铺	diànpù	*n.*	shop; store	50
订单	dìngdān	*n.*	purchase order	53
逗	dòu	*v.*	tease; kid	11
独生子女	dúshēng zǐnǚ		only child	2
短暂	duǎnzàn	*adj.*	of short duration	97

词语	拼音	词性	含义	页码
墩买里	Dūnmǎilǐ	*p.n.*	name of a place	54
多面手	duōmiànshǒu	*n.*	jack-of-all-trades; versatile person	105
儿媳	érxí	*n.*	daughter-in-law	76
二胎	èrtāi	*n.*	second child	6
发小	fàxiǎo	*n.*	childhood buddy	47
翻地	fāndì	*v.*	turn up the soil	67
繁荣	fánróng	*adj.*	flourishing; prosperous	139
方	fāng	*n.*	side; party	5
放鞭炮	fàng biānpào		set off firecrackers	75
放开	fàngkāi	*v.*	loosen	6
分店	fēndiàn	*n.*	branch (of a shop)	54
风向标	fēngxiàngbiāo	*n.*	weathercock	105
夫妻	fūqī	*n.*	husband and wife	2
赶上	gǎnshàng	*v.*	be in time for	9
干练	gànliàn	*adj.*	capable and experienced	44
钢琴	gāngqín	*n.*	piano	136
高端	gāoduān	*n.*	high-end	127
高徒	gāotú	*n.*	outstanding disciple	121
公交	gōngjiāo	*n.*	public transport	33
功底	gōngdǐ	*n.*	basic training; foundation	123
供品	gòngpǐn	*n.*	offering	74
供桌	gòngzhuō	*n.*	altar table	72
孤单	gūdān	*adj.*	alone; lonely	9
瓜子儿	guāzǐr	*n.*	melon seed	80
挂历	guàlì	*n.*	wall calendar	73
国策	guócè	*n.*	state/national policy	5
寒风	hánfēng	*n.*	cold/bleak wind	33
寒暄	hánxuān	*v.*	exchange (conventional) greetings	88

词语	拼音	词性	含义	页码
好评	hǎopíng	*n.*	favourable comment; good review	118
核桃	hétao	*n.*	walnut	49
后半夜	hòubànyè	*n.*	after midnight	106
护肤霜	hùfūshuāng	*n.*	face cream; body lotion	25
缓解	huǎnjiě	*v.*	alleviate; ease up	35
回单	huídān	*n.*	receipt	29
回赠	huízèng	*v.*	give sb a gift in return	87
货架	huòjià	*n.*	goods shelf	50
积攒	jīzǎn	*v.*	collect/save bit by bit	98
急促	jícù	*adj.*	hurried; rapid	79
集	jí	*n.*	country fair; market	71
计划生育	jìhuà shēngyù		family planning	5
祭祀	jìsì	*v.*	offer sacrifices to gods/ancestors	72
假期	jiàqī	*n.*	holiday; vacation; break	54
兼任	jiānrèn	*v.*	hold a concurrent post	101
捡拾	jiǎnshí	*v.*	collect; gather	64
简易	jiǎnyì	*adj.*	simply equipped	102
间断	jiànduàn	*v.*	be disconnected	47
间隙	jiànxì	*n.*	interval; gap	29
奖项	jiǎngxiàng	*n.*	prize	101
奖状	jiǎngzhuàng	*n.*	certificate of merit/award	73
饺子	jiǎozi	*n.*	*jiaozi*; Chinese dumpling	74
脚丫	jiǎoyā	*n.*	foot	12
轿车	jiàochē	*n.*	car	84
教学	jiàoxué	*n.*	teaching; education	47
结伴	jiébàn	*v.*	go with	71
解乏	jiěfá	*v.*	recover from fatigue	34
解题	jiětí	*v.*	solve a (mathematical, etc) problem	47

J

词语	拼音	词性	含义	页码
金钱	jīnqián	*n.*	money	130
近期	jìnqī	*n.*	near future; recent days	26
近亲	jìnqīn	*n.*	close relative	83
精英	jīngyīng	*n.*	elite	130
酒席	jiǔxí	*n.*	feast; banquet	88
就算	jiùsuàn	*conj.*	even if	68
剧情	jùqíng	*n.*	plot of a play/an opera	97
据	jù	*prep.*	according to	30
均衡	jūnhéng	*adj.*	balanced; proportionate	5
K 开机	kāijī	*v.*	(of a film, etc) start shooting	109
课堂	kètáng	*n.*	classroom	106
快递	kuàidì	*n.*	special/express delivery	23
快件	kuàijiàn	*n.*	express mail/delivery	26
L 垃圾	lājī	*n.*	rubbish; garbage	88
腊月	làyuè	*n.*	twelfth month of the lunar year	67
来访	láifǎng	*v.*	come to visit	83
老板	lǎobǎn	*n.*	boss	36
老伴儿	lǎobànr	*n.*	(of an old couple) husband or wife	76
姥爷	lǎoye	*n.*	(maternal) grandfather	14
礼品	lǐpǐn	*n.*	present; gift	87
临产	línchǎn	*v.*	be about to give birth	2
零售	língshòu	*v.*	retail; sell by retail	53
刘燚	Liú Yì	*p.n.*	name of a person	97
遛	liù	*v.*	walk leisurely; stroll	71
录像机	lùxiàngjī	*n.*	video recorder	98
录影	lùyǐng	*v.*	videotape; record	100
录制	lùzhì	*v.*	record; video	105
路程	lùchéng	*n.*	distance travelled; journey	26

词语	拼音	词性	含义	页码
路灯	lùdēng	*n.*	streetlight; street/road lamp	68
落户	luòhù	*v.*	settle (down)	118
M 满月	mǎnyuè	*v.*	(of a baby) be one month old	2
每当	měidāng	*prep.*	whenever; every time	33
美好	měihǎo	*adj.*	(of life, future, wish, etc) fine; glorious	121
美味	měiwèi	*n.*	fine food; table delicacies	49
萌芽	méngyá	*v.*	bud; germinate	98
梦想	mèngxiǎng	*n.*	dream	36
面粉	miànfěn	*n.*	(wheat) flour	53
民国	Mínguó	*p.n.*	Republic of China (1912 ~ 1949)	117
民俗	mínsú	*n.*	folk custom	50
明确	míngquè	*adj.*	clear and definite	139
抹	mǒ	*v.*	apply; put on	25
N 奶茶	nǎichá	*n.*	milk tea	54
馕	náng	*n.*	crusty pancake (staple food of the Uygur and Kazak ethnic groups)	49
内斗	nèidòu	*v.*	internal conflict	124
腻	nì	*adj.*	bored of; fed up with	57
年画	niánhuà	*n.*	Spring Festival picture	73
农耕	nónggēng	*n.*	farming	67
农活儿	nónghuór	*n.*	farm work	67
P 趴	pā	*v.*	lie on one's stomach	76
拍摄	pāishè	*v.*	shoot; photograph	100
派件	pàijiàn	*v.*	ship; deliver	29
潘庄	Pānzhuāng	*p.n.*	name of a village	64
泡脚	pàojiǎo	*v.*	soak feet in warm water	34
泡面	pàomiàn	*n.*	instant noodles	29
陪伴	péibàn	*v.*	keep sb company	5
陪护	péihù	*v.*	accompany and look after	2

词语	拼音	词性	含义	页码
蓬勃	péngbó	*adj.*	flourishing; thriving	23
批量	pīliàng	*adv.*	in batches/bulk	127
疲劳	píláo	*adj.*	tired; fatigued	35
拼凑	pīncòu	*v.*	put/piece together	64
评判	píngpàn	*v.*	judge; determine	128
评委	píngwěi	*n.*	member of a review committee; judge	100
凭借	píngjiè	*v.*	rely on; depend on	123
Q 起色	qǐsè	*n.*	improvement; pickup	50
气息	qìxī	*n.*	smell; flavour; scent	44
契机	qìjī	*n.*	turning point; juncture	118
前行	qiánxíng	*v.*	go/move forward	68
墙壁	qiángbì	*n.*	wall	102
清扫	qīngsǎo	*v.*	thoroughly clean up	80
圈	quān	*n.*	circle	109
R 热衷	rèzhōng	*v.*	be keen on; have a burning passion for	130
人家	rénjiā	*n.*	household	79
人手	rénshǒu	*n.*	manpower; hand	50
肉乎乎	ròuhūhū	*adj.*	chubby	9
乳名	rǔmíng	*n.*	infant name	2
入神	rùshén	*v.*	be entranced	76
S 散落	sànluò	*v.*	fall scattered	80
上交	shàngjiāo	*v.*	hand in; submit	29
上映	shàngyìng	*v.*	release; show (a film)	105
深厚	shēnhòu	*adj.*	solid; deep-seated	123
失传	shīchuán	*v.*	be lost; no longer exist	123
十足	shízú	*adj.*	sheer; downright	139
食材	shícái	*n.*	ingredient; food	72
史料	shǐliào	*n.*	historical data/materials	124

词语	拼音	词性	含义	页码
试验品	shìyànpǐn	*n.*	experimental sample	50
室外	shìwài	*n.*	outside of a building	25
首肯	shǒukěn	*v.*	approve	100
售卖	shòumài	*v.*	sell	50
碎片	suìpiàn	*n.*	fragment; piece	64
昙华林	Tánhuálín	*p.n.*	name of a place	118
弹	tán	*v.*	play (a musical instrument)	136
堂哥	tánggē	*n.*	cousin	75
讨	tǎo	*v.*	ask/beg for	71
讨说法	tǎo shuōfǎ		demand an explanation	124
天马行空	tiānmǎ-xíngkōng		like a heavenly steed soaring across the skies—(of writing, calligraphy, etc) powerful and unconstrained in style	121
添置	tiānzhì	*v.*	add to one's possessions	100
甜蜜	tiánmì	*adj.*	sweet; happy	30
帖子	tiězi	*n.*	posting	127
停滞不前	tíngzhì-bùqián		remain stagnant	133
同胞	tóngbāo	*n.*	sibling	2
头部	tóubù	*n.*	head	35
投射	tóushè	*v.*	project; cast	102
推搡	tuīsǎng	*v.*	push; decline	87
退隐	tuìyǐn	*v.*	(of an official) retire from public life	128
崴	wǎi	*v.*	sprain; twist	106
外孙女	wàisūnnǚ	*n.*	daughter's daughter; granddaughter	9
微电影	wēidiànyǐng	*n.*	short film	98
问世	wènshì	*v.*	come out	123
舞台	wǔtái	*n.*	stage; arena	14
舞台剧	wǔtáijù	*n.*	stage play	97

词语	拼音	词性	含义	页码
物流业	wùliúyè	n.	logistics industry	23
习惯性	xíguànxìng	n.	habituation	30
袭	xí	m.	a suit or set of clothes	44
下	xià	v.	put into; cook	34
闲谈	xiántán	v.	chat	84
乡邻	xiānglín	n.	fellow villager	83
香甜	xiāngtián	adj.	sound (sleep)	12
享受	xiǎngshòu	v.	enjoy	34
小大人儿	xiǎodàrénr	n.	child talking or behaving like an adult	9
小有名气	xiǎoyǒu-míngqì		have some reputation	49
兴起	xīngqǐ	v.	rise; spring up	23
行李	xíngli	n.	luggage; baggage	68
兄弟姐妹	xiōngdì jiěmèi		brothers and sisters; siblings	5
绣坊	xiùfáng	n.	embroidery workshop	121
绣线	xiùxiàn	n.	thread	135
叙旧	xùjiù	v.	talk about the past	83
轩	xuān	n.	small room or veranda with windows (used in names of studios, restaurants or teahouses in ancient times)	117
渲染	xuànrǎn	v.	apply colours to a drawing	127
学者	xuézhě	n.	scholar	124
压力	yālì	n.	pressure; stress	54
烟花	yānhuā	n.	fireworks	79
延迟	yánchí	v.	delay; postpone	33
研制	yánzhì	v.	develop; prepare	57
演播室	yǎnbōshì	n.	studio	105
扬州	Yángzhōu	p.n.	a city in Jiangsu Province	23
液晶彩电	yèjīng cǎidiàn		liquid crystal TV	76

词语	拼音	词性	含义	页码
医疗	yīliáo	*n.*	medical care	57
一瘸一拐	yìqué-yìguǎi		walk with a limp	106
迎宾	yíngbīn	*v.*	greet/welcome guests	80
营养	yíngyǎng	*n.*	nutrition; nourishment	49
影评	yǐngpíng	*n.*	film review	105
影视	yǐngshì	*n.*	film and television	73
油画	yóuhuà	*n.*	oil painting	123
游针绣	yóuzhēnxiù	*n.*	a way of needling	123
袁梓馨	Yuán Zǐxīn	*p.n.*	name of a person	2
原本	yuánběn	*adv.*	originally; formerly	130
援建	yuánjiàn	*v.*	provide aid in construction	53
院线	yuànxiàn	*n.*	theatre chain; cinema	105
院子	yuànzi	*n.*	courtyard	136
炸裂	zhàliè	*v.*	explode; blow up	79
展销会	zhǎnxiāohuì	*n.*	commodities fair	53
张罗	zhāngluo	*v.*	plan and prepare	88
招徒	zhāotú	*v.*	recruit apprentice	121
照看	zhàokàn	*v.*	attend to; look after	54
针法	zhēnfǎ	*n.*	stitch	123
针织	zhēnzhī	*v.*	knit	127
振冉	Zhènrǎn	*p.n.*	name of a person	83
正月	zhēngyuè	*n.*	first month of the lunar year	84
正餐	zhèngcān	*n.*	regular meal	29
正轨	zhèngguǐ	*n.*	right track	50
正统	zhèngtǒng	*n.*	legitimism	124
知名度	zhīmíngdù	*n.*	popularity	118

词语	拼音	词性	含义	页码
知性	zhīxìng	*n.*	intellectuality	44
职	zhí	*n.*	post; office	101
制片	zhìpiàn	*n.*	producer; film maker	101
质疑	zhìyí	*v.*	call in question; query	124
住所	zhùsuǒ	*n.*	dwelling place; residence	117
注资	zhùzī	*v.*	inject capital	50
专注	zhuānzhù	*v.*	be concentrated	133
撰写	zhuànxiě	*v.*	write (usually short articles)	100
走动	zǒudòng	*v.*	(of relatives and friends) visit each other	88
走亲访友	zǒuqīn-fǎngyǒu		visit one's relatives and friends	84
租金	zūjīn	*n.*	rent	53
足迹	zújì	*n.*	footprint; track	109
组合	zǔhé	*n.*	combination	6
做客	zuòkè	*v.*	be a guest/visitor	88